Fascinating Indian Folk Tales

Retold By:
Swapna Dutta

Illustrated By:
Jishu Dev Malakar

PANDA
An imprint of Unicorn Books

Contents

Foreword

India is a storehouse of folk tales. They have been passed down by word of mouth from one generation to the next. The stories cover every subject under the sun – from tales of wisdom to humour; every state has its own special tales. In fact, many of these stories are common to several states with just local variations. That is why it is difficult to say which state they originally belong to. Hence, it is best to consider them as just Indian folk tales.

ISBN 978-81-7806-092-7

UNICORN BOOKS Pvt Ltd.

J-3/16, Darya Ganj, New Delhi-110002
Phones: 23276539,23272783/84, Fax: 23257790,
E mail: unicornbooks@vsnl.com • www.unicornbooks.in

The Magical Chant

"So today is the last day!" said Ajit, tying up his things in a neat bundle.

"Yes, it is," said Prince Ashish, looking out of the window at the green fields beyond. "And we'll be home, all of us, with new things to do."

Both were at the *gurukula* to complete their education. There, in the peaceful surroundings of the woods, princes and paupers lived under the same roof, learning things from their *guru* and forgetting all their social differences. That is how Ajit, the grocer's son and Prince Ashish were friends. Despite being a prince, Ashish was neither sharp nor shrewd. He was basically a scholar with an artistic temperament. He trusted everyone. Everyone was a friend to him. He considered Ajit to be his dear friend because he seemed devoted to him. Ashish himself was straightforward and he did not suspect slyness or dishonesty in anyone else.

"It makes me really sad to think that we may never see each other again," said Ajit, "unless we visit each other."

"I am sure we will," said Ashish. "You'll always be welcome in my house."

"And you in mine," said Ajit. "Why don't you visit my house first before you go off to your palace?"

"I will, if you want me to," said Ashish.

The two friends set off for Ajit's house the next day and reached there just before sunset. Ajit asked Ashish to wait outside while he went in to call his parents. He said they would love to welcome him properly. Ashish stood under a tree waiting to be called in. But minutes passed. Ashish was puzzled and wondered if his friend had forgotten him in all the excitement of home-coming. Then suddenly, he heard voices. Ajit's parents came out accompanied by his brother, sister and Ajit himself.

"Who is that boy?" asked Ajit's mother pointing at Ashish.

"And what is he doing there under the tree?" asked Ajit's father, frowning.

"Oh! I forgot to tell you about him," said Ajit. "He is the new servant I just engaged and brought along with me!"

"A servant?" Ajit's father frowned. "We don't need anyone! What work can he do?"

"Nothing much, if you ask me," said Ajit. "But I felt sorry for the poor fellow and asked him to come along. He can at least cut the grass for our cattle."

"He looks too handsome and refined for a servant," said Ajit's sister. "Where did you pick him up?"

"Don't worry your head about him," said Ajit with a laugh. "Besides, looks can be deceptive."

"He looks hungry," Ajit's mother looked at Ashish's tired face. "I'll give him something to eat first. I've already cooked all your favourite dishes for you."

"Don't spoil him, mother," said Ajit. "Give him plain puffed rice. That's good enough for a servant!"

"And give him some work to do soon afterwards," said Ajit's father. "I won't have any lazybones in my house!"

Poor Ashish was too stunned to believe his own ears. But he soon realised it was no joke and he had fallen into a wicked trap laid by his friend. But he decided to say nothing for the time being.

"Here," said Ajit, throwing him the sickle. "Go and cut grass for our cows!"

Ashish picked up the sickle without a word and made his way for the field. He wondered at first if he could run away to his own home. Then he remembered that Ajit had carried the box containing all his money and princely clothes inside, along with his own. He had absolutely nothing, not even money to travel anywhere or send a message to his own people. Besides, it would be cowardly to run away.

Ashish decided to stay and see things through. But he felt very depressed by the thought that he had been so badly betrayed by his friend. He was so completely lost in his thoughts that the sickle slipped from his hand, cutting a finger in half. Ashish groaned as he saw the blood gushing out. The pain was more than he could bear.

Just at that moment, Lord Shiva and Parvati were returning to heaven after a tour of the world. As the ethereal chariot cut across the clouds, Parvati heard Ashish groaning with pain, way down below. "What is that, my Lord?" she asked Lord Shiva. "Who is moaning in pain?"

"A lad let down by his friend," answered Lord Shiva.

"Let us go to him for a moment," pleaded Parvati.

"Very well, if that is what you wish," Lord Shiva stopped his chariot and both of them walked up to Ashish.

"What is the matter, my son?" asked Parvati.

"Just an accident, mother," said Ashish, wondering, who the angelic couple could be.

"Anyone to blame for this?" asked Shiva, looking at him keenly. "Have you been wronged?"

"Oh, no, sir," said Ashish at once. "Just my own carelessness."

"I'll teach you a magical chant to mend your finger," said Parvati. "Just hold it together and say:

For Shiva's sake

Hold fast and strong.

Till I say so,

Hold hard and long!"

"This chant will firmly join anything, including your cut finger," said Shiva. Before the astonished Ashish could say a word, the divine couple just vanished!

Ashish blinked his eyes and wondered if he had been dreaming. His finger was bleeding as badly as ever. He decided to try the chant. He said it, and lo and behold! It healed as though the accident had never happened! There was no bleeding and pain! Ashish blinked again and guessed that Lord Shiva himself along with Parvati had come down to help him.

*****

For a whole month, Ashish lived with Ajit, working like a servant. He did not speak to Ajit at all. And Ajit, feeling uncomfortable and ill at ease, avoided him. He had originally meant it as a joke, quite expecting Ashish to flare up and disclose his identity at once. But when Ashish did not speak, Ajit was tempted to continue the game and lord over him. He had always been jealous of him and this seemed an excellent opportunity to make him suffer. And now, there seemed to be no way of ending the wicked game, he had started. He wondered if Ashish intended to pay him back.

Ashish did intend it. Not so much to "pay him back", but to teach him that dishonesty and disloyalty do not pay. He soon got his chance. One morning, as Ajit sat in the sun, his sister brought him a bowl of milk. Ashish was sweeping the floor. He looked up and saw Ajit sipping from the bowl. Ashish recited the magical chant softly. The bowl stuck to Ajit's lips at once! He jumped up in surprise and tried to pull it off. It was of no use. The bowl stuck to his lips as if it was a part of his face! Ajit tried to shout, but only a gurgling sound came from his lips!

Ajit jumped about the place, making strange noises. His sister heard him and came running. "Why are you biting the bowl like that?" she asked in surprise. Ajit tried to speak, but couldn't.

"Give me that bowl," said his sister, trying to pull it away. Ashish saw her catch the bowl and repeated the chant. Instantly, her hand also stuck to the bowl. She howled wildly and asked Ashish to fetch her parents at once.

Ajit's father was busy when Ashish went to him and said that his son and daughter wanted him urgently. He frowned but got up and went home. When he saw Ajit and his sister struggling with the bowl, he thought they were merely playing. He boxed Ajit's ears but was unable to move his hand away! Ashish, watching the fun, had repeated the chant quietly!

After some time, Ajit's mother burst upon the scene with a rolling pin in hand. "What is all the noise about? And good heavens! What do you mean by pulling my poor child's ears?" She tried to pull away her husband's hand but to her horror, found her own hand stuck fast to his! She screamed and shouted! Ajit's little brother came running and tried to pull his mother's hand but found his hand stuck firmly to hers.

The old cook came out of the kitchen. "For shame!" she said, as she saw the whole family struggling hard to unclasp. "Fighting like cats and dogs! That too at your age!" she cried.

The cook tried to pull her mistress away and got stuck to her instead! There was utter chaos!

"It must be witchcraft!" shouted Ajit's mother.

"Or ghosts!" screamed the cook.

"What are we to do?" shouted Ajit's father, looking puzzled and angry.

Ashish was the only one, who was not affected by this 'witchcraft' – and naturally so! But strangely enough, no one suspected him of playing a trick. Finally, Ajit's father decided that they should send for the family priest and seek his advice. He asked Ashish to fetch the priest immediately.

It was almost midnight when Ashish reached the priest's house. By then, it was raining heavily. The priest was not at all pleased to be disturbed at this hour.

"Whatever the matter is, it can wait till morning," he said yawning.

"But, sir, it is most urgent," insisted Ashish. "The master told me to bring you at once."

"Must be a wedding or a feast of some kind!" said the priest's wife coming into the room. "I expect they want you to perform the rites."

"What is it, boy?" asked the priest frowning.

"I was merely asked to bring you back with me, sir," said Ashish.

"You'd better go," said the priest's wife, "and I shall come, too!"

"You?" cried the priest. "At night, and in this rain? Don't be crazy, woman!"

"I am coming," said the priest's wife in a determined voice. "You are always leaving me out of feasts and fun. I'm not going to miss this one!"

"But I don't know if this is a feast," said the priest grumbling. "The boy doesn't say so."

"Well, it isn't a death in the family!" argued his wife. "Is anyone dead, boy?"

"No, madam," said Ashish truthfully.

"There you are!" cried the priest's wife triumphantly. "It must be a wedding then! I am coming."

It was still raining hard when the three of them started with Ashish leading the way. He suddenly stopped before a puddle. "There is a big puddle here. Madam will get very wet!" he said.

"Well, what do you expect me to do?" shouted the priest. "Carry her?"

"You could put her on your back for a moment and jump across," suggested Ashish. "It's just a step!"

"Now, that's a really clever idea!" said the priest's wife. "I hate walking through puddles and my sari will get quite spoilt."

The priest muttered under his breath and took his wife on his back. Ashish chuckled and whispered the chant. "Now get off from my back," shouted the priest after crossing the puddle. "I can't think why you tagged along all the way in this rain!"

"I can't get off," said his wife. "I'm stuck!"

As no amount of shouting, cursing, or pleading was of any use, the poor priest had to walk all the way carrying his wife on his back. Ajit and his people had been anxiously awaiting the priest. They burst out laughing when they saw him come in with his wife on his back. How they laughed!

"It's kind of you to have come!" said Ajit's father. "But why are you carrying madam on your back, now that you are safely home? Do ask her to get down!"

"I have told her a number of times but the stupid woman simply refuses to!" said the priest in an angry voice.

"Please, madam, won't you get down from *guruji's* back now that you are here?" said Ajit's father, trying not to laugh.

"I've told you I can't," said the priest's wife. "I'm stuck!"

Ajit's father frowned. "You seem to be in the same mess as the rest of us," he said at last.

"But how can such a thing happen?" fumed the priest. "Someone must know something about it! Ask this servant of yours!" Then it dawned on everyone that Ashish alone was free from any trouble. Ajit's father begged him to tell the truth. "I know that somehow you are behind all this. Perhaps, we have wronged you in some way. Do please tell us everything."

Ashish told them the whole story. He then took back the magical chant and freed them from the spell. Everyone begged his pardon, especially the shame-faced Ajit. Ashish forgave them readily but he left for his home, the very same day.

Rumna and Jhumna

Once upon a time, there lived a poor man, who had two daughters, Rumna and Jhumna. Their mother had died when they were little girls and they had a stepmother, who hated them, although, she had no children of her own.

Rumna and Jhumna worked all day long, doing all the housework and helping their father look after the few cattle owned by them. One morning, the stepmother told them that there was nothing to eat at home. If they wanted a meal, they should go into the forest and get some wild herbs and fruits. Rumna and Jhumna knew that it was no use arguing with her. They left quietly taking a basket with them. Jhumna, the younger sister was crying because she was very hungry.

"Don't cry Jhumna dear," said Rumna, trying to comfort her. "I am sure we will find some nice juicy fruits in the forest and you can have as many as you want."

"There will be no fruits in this season," said Jhumna. "You know that as well as I do. I know, we shall starve to death. That's what our new mother wants, anyway."

"Don't say that," said Rumna. "We are sure to find something. Come, walk faster, the sun is getting hotter by the minute."

"If only the sun could help us!" sighed Jhumna. As the sisters walked deeper and deeper into the forest, the sunlight grew dim. There were huge trees standing close together that made the place seem quite dark.

"Let's go back," said Jhumna with a shiver. "There isn't any fruit or berry to be found and I feel afraid in this dim light. What if wild animals come and attack us?"

Rumna thought the same. "Very well," she said looking around her. "Do you remember which road we had taken while coming? The left one or the right one?"

Jhumna couldn't remember either. They had lost their way and walked deeper and deeper into the forest.

Suddenly, they saw a beam of light ahead. "That must be the way out of the forest," said Rumna eagerly. "Come, let's go that way."

They walked towards the light and soon found themselves inside a well-kept garden with a big pond. A group of beautiful girls sat in a ring worshipping.

"They must be *devakanyas* or damsels from heaven," whispered Rumna. "Look at their rainbow-coloured wings! They are worshipping the **sun.** I had heard they do it during this time of the year. Shhh.... we mustn't disturb them."

The sisters hid quietly behind the trees and watched the damsels worshipping the sun. After the rituals were complete, they flew away like birds.

Rumna had a bright idea. "Come Jhumna, let us also worship the sun. Perhaps, he will listen to our prayers and end our miseries."

"But we don't know how," said Jhumna.

"We have just watched how they did it, didn't we? Let's do it the same way."

So Rumna and Jhumna gathered some wild flowers and made a pitcher out of mud just as they had seen the *devakanyas* do. Then they took a dip in the pond and worshipped the sun.

"My Lord, Sun, the giver of light and life, we offer you our homage. Please accept it and give us your blessings," said Rumna.

"Lord Sun, please take away our problems and let us be happy," said Jhumna.

A bright beam of sunlight fell on their pitchers but nothing else happened. When they stood up, however, they suddenly found their way home. What's more, the road, that had seemed so long in the morning, seemed a short one now.

*****

A big surprise awaited them when they reached home. Their poor hut had vanished. A lovely villa with a garden stood in its place, complete with a pond and grazing ground for the cattle. The house was full of beautiful things and everything, one could wish for! Rumna and Jhumna were delighted and knew that it was the sun, who had blessed them with all these riches and prosperity. Their father was delighted too. But their stepmother was very jealous. All these riches and beautiful things made her more greedy and finally, she made a plan to get rid of Rumna and Jhumna. She commanded her husband to take them away to the forest and leave them there.

"Now that we are so rich and have everything we want, I don't want them here," she said. She made life so miserable for the poor man that he gave in ultimately.

"Rumna and Jhumna, get ready early tomorrow morning. I shall take you to your aunt's place."

"We never knew we had an aunt, father!" said Rumna. "You never told us about her before."

"Didn't I? Oh well, I mu....must have forgotten," said their father, stammering with embarrassment. He hated deceiving his daughters but he knew that his wife would give him no peace until he did what she said.

The girls were up and ready early the next morning. "Jhumna, don't forget to carry our pitchers with which we worship the sun," said Rumna. "We must carry on worshipping him wherever we are, since he has been so good and kind to us."

Their father took them deep inside the forest. "How much longer is it?" asked Jhumna, who was very tired.

"I am so thirsty," said Rumna, "there doesn't seem to be any pond in sight."

"Wait under this tree while I get some water for you," said their father. The girls were so tired that they soon fell asleep. Their father left them there and rushed back home.

When Rumna woke up, it was pitch dark. Worse, their father was nowhere in sight. The place was covered with long bushes and thick and tall trees, suffocating the frightened Rumna. "Wake up, Jhumna," she said, shaking her sister.

"What's up? Where's father? Has he left us alone and gone back home?" said Jhumna, rubbing her eyes.

"Looks like it," said Rumna with a shiver. "This forest is full of wild beasts. I hope they won't attack us in the night." However, this time, the younger sister, Jhumna gathered all her courage and consoled Rumna.

"Let us worship the good sun once again," said Jhumna. "I am sure he will protect us and the good Lord will understand our terrible plight and surely find out a way to help us get out of this thick jungle before it is too late.

The sisters placed the sacred pitchers before them and prayed that the sun might protect them and look after them, now that they were totally on their own left out at the hands of destiny.

Almost immediately, they caught sight of a little house atop a tall tree nearby and a ladder propped in front of it. The sisters climbed up and found themselves in a cosy shelter with food and clothes and even a bed to sleep in.

"It is the sun looking after us once again," said Jhumna.

"I am not afraid anymore," said Rumna. "I can feel something good will happen to us!"

And she was right! A prince, who had come hunting in the forest with his friend, the minister's son, found them in the morning and took them home in his chariot. The king and queen were so charmed by their beauty that they got Rumna married to the prince and Jhumna to his friend. And so the sisters lived happily ever after.

Can you guess what happened to their father? As soon as he reached home after leaving his daughters in the forest, he found himself in his old broken shack with no trace of the riches that the sun had given them. Everything had vanished the moment Rumna and Jhumna walked out with the pitchers, they had made for worshipping the sun! This is because cruelty and selfishness can never bring prosperity and happiness.

The Rainbow Prince

Princess Rupanjali was indeed a vision of beauty. Her smile held the colours of the rainbow. Her teeth were like pearls. When she walked, roses seemed to bloom beneath her feet. When she sang, the birds sang too. Her voice was like the song of the cuckoo. Her laughter was like the babbling brook. She dazzled every eye. "What a beautiful girl!" said the people of the land and everyone, who happened to see her.

The king, her father, looked at her and grew pensive. Where would he find a prince good enough for her? The queen looked at her and sighed. To whom would she entrust this beautiful lass? Princess Rupanjali, unaware of their anxiety, laughed and sang and grew prettier and prettier each day. Her friends and playmates adored her. The most devoted and loyal among them was Nilanjana. She was a simple peasant girl, gentle and kind. She often envied the beautiful princess whose world was as lovely as a dream.

But beauty is not the only thing in life. Princess Rupanjali was extremely proud and unkind, despite her ravishing looks. She would have nothing ugly or old. And she could not bear to be scolded, criticised or denied a single wish. She ruled her little world with a firm hand, insisting on getting her own way in everything.

One morning, a strange thing happened. The king was in his court listening to the problems of the people when the entire hall was suddenly filled with the most exquisite music, they had ever heard. Everyone turned around to see a stranger playing on a harp. His white robe shone like moonbeams. There was a garland of jasmine flowers around his neck. His harp was snow-white too.

"I have come from the Land of Rainbows," he said in a voice as sweet as his harp.

"Have you come on a special mission?" the king asked him.

"Yes, I have," he answered with a smile. "I have been sent by the Rainbow Prince, who is the best-looking prince on earth. We are looking for a bride, who will be good enough for him. He has heard of Princess Rupanjali and has sent me as his messenger to convey his proposal."

The king got up from his throne and clasped the hands of the messenger.

"My heartiest welcome to you," he said. "I cannot tell you how happy I am to know that my daughter is lucky enough to be selected by the Rainbow Prince himself."

The messenger smiled and said, "But there is an important thing, I have not told you as yet. A wicked old witch, who came to our land in disguise, has put the Rainbow Prince to sleep. She has breathed the consciousness of the prince into a blood-red parrot, who has flown away. He will not regain consciousness until the bird is found."

"In that case, we just have to find the bird," said the king, looking worried. "I only hope it will not prove to be an impossible task."

*****

The news spread throughout the land. It reached the ears of the soldiers, the farmers, the workers and the people at large. It reached the ears of the queen, resting in her chamber and also the ears of Princess Rupanjali, seated in her garden among her friends. She left her bower in a hurry and went to the king.

"I must have the red parrot, father," she said in a determined voice.

The king looked at her with amused eyes. "We do not know where it has flown, child. We shall try, but it looks like an impossible task to me."

Princess Rupanjali stamped her foot impatiently. "I don't want excuses. I must have the bird! I am not going to marry anyone but the Rainbow Prince."

The king looked at her in despair. He knew that she would stick to her words. Rupanjali looked at his worried face and said, "Let every single bird in the kingdom be caught. The red parrot is bound to be among them."

There was a faint murmur in the court. It seemed such an unkind thing to do. But the princess was firm. "Whoever is careless and allows a single bird to go free will die in consequence," she announced in a loud voice.

The king endorsed her words half-heartedly. He wished heartily that she were a little less beautiful and a little kinder!

The trapping of birds started the very next day. The entire kingdom was overcrowded with various kinds of nets and traps. Not a bird sang amongst the trees, and none flew across the sky. The nests were all deserted.

A special bird-prison had been made for the trapped birds. There were thousands of them. The entire cell resounded with their heart-rending, frightened cries.

Nilanjana heard them with tears in her eyes. Her heart went out to the poor birds. She decided to go to Princess Rupanjali and plead for their freedom. Surely, she would understand. Nilanjana went to the royal chamber of the princess and fell at her feet. "Oh, do set the poor birds free, dear princess," she sobbed. "Don't you see how wretched they are? Princess, how can you find your life's happiness by giving such pain to the poor creatures?"

Princess Rupanjali's eyes flashed dangerously as she pushed Nilanjana off her feet. "Here speaks the merciful one!" she said sarcastically. "Is there anyone around? Take her away and imprison her with the birds since she loves them so much."

Instantly, the royal guards appeared and dragged Nilanjana to the bird-prison. Princess Rupanjali looked at her and laughed a cruel laugh.

Nilanjana was pushed into a corner of the bird-prison where she cried herself to sleep. Just before dawn, she was suddenly awakened. Someone was calling her in a soft, sweet voice. She opened her eyes to find a little red bird speaking to her.

"Do set me free, Nilanjana," it said in a soft voice. "How cruel you human beings are! Just see how the chain has bruised my wings and I am starving. Set me free or I shall die."

"You poor darling!" said Nilanjana and kissed the little bird. "How you have suffered! I will break off your chains. I don't care what happens to me." She tried with all her strength and skill to break the chains without hurting the bird. At last, after hours of patient labour, she set it free with sore and bleeding hands.

In the meantime, Princess Rupanjali got the news that a red parrot had been caught. She dashed into the prison only to see it flying away from Nilanjana's hands. She stamped her feet and let out a wild shriek.

"You wicked, wretched girl! How dare you set my parrot free! You shall die for it. I swear!"

Nilanjana clasped her hands in remorse. "Do forgive me, princess," she said. "I had not realised that it was the very parrot, you were looking for. I couldn't bear its suffering. Indeed, it would have surely died if I had not set it free when I did."

At Rupanjali's command, Nilanjana was taken to the top of a hill. From there, she would be thrown into the gushing waterfall far down below. The tears, pleadings and entreaties of the people left the princess completely cold. Even the king and the queen could not change her decision. Nilanjana had released the precious red parrot and she must die, thought the cruel princess.

Rupanjali stood watching as they gave Nilanjana a push, but as she was about to fall, a pair of strong arms rescued her. Trembling with shock and relief, Nilanjana looked up to see the handsomest man, she had ever seen.

"I am the Rainbow Prince," he said and gently put her on the ground.

"How wonderful for our princess that you are well again," Nilanjana said, smiling with real happiness. "Perhaps, she will forgive me now. Where is the dear little red bird?"

The Rainbow Prince merely laughed. Then he took off his garland and placed it around Nilanjana's neck.

"What does this mean?" Nilanjana asked, bewildered. "Don't you know that I am not Princess Rupanjali? I am only a poor peasant girl."

"You are now my queen," said the prince with a smile. "That story about the Red Parrot was only a test. Princess Rupanjali may be far more beautiful than you are. But in kindness, bravery, loyalty and things that really count in life, you are far ahead."

Then he placed Nilanjana on his golden chariot and rode towards the Land of Rainbows.

How Was The Moon Created?

Many, many years ago, when the world was newly created, there was only the glowing sun shining in the azure to give light to the people. Time consisted of an infinite day with the sun remaining brightly all the time in the sky.

The sun did not set at all. So there was nothing called night. People worked until they were too tired to work any more. Then they stopped to rest. There was no set time for work or a fixed time for sleep.

One day, the Creator came to monitor the world. He saw some men working in the fields. "When did you plough this field?" he asked one of them.

"Today," replied the man looking at the Creator in surprise.

"When did you dig that pit?" the Creator asked another.

"Today," said the second man.

"And when did you make that garden?"

"Today, of course," said the third man looking puzzled. "Why do you ask, my Lord? There is only today! Whatever happens, happens today."

The Creator said nothing but simply walked on. He met a woman carrying a little child in her arms.

"When was this boy born?" he asked the mother.

"Today, master," said the woman, bowing low.

Before long, the other children also came there and stood by their mother.

"And when were their siblings born?" the creator asked again.

"Today, of course," said the woman in surprise. "Why do you ask such a strange question? Everything happens today."

Then the Creator understood. The people had no sense of time because there was no bifurcation of days and nights, no division of time. He decided to do something about it. He called out to the sun and said, "You must not remain in the sky all the time."

"Then what should I do, master?" asked the sun in surprise.

"You must set in the evening and rise again, the next morning. Then the people will not work when it is dark and know that it is the time for resting. When you rise again, they will know that it is another day, not the same one."

"Very well, master," said the sun. "It shall be as you wish."

*****

The next day, as soon as it was evening, the sun went down and the world grew dark. The people did not understand what had happened or why it was dark. They were frightened and ran amuck. Some of them fell into ditches and hurt themselves. Some children fell from trees. The women knocked their vessels in the dark and broke them. There was total confusion everywhere. Nobody knew what to do!

Finally, the oldest man, the wizard among them, called out to everyone and said, "Lie down and rest, all of you. You can do nothing in this darkness."

Gradually, people learned to think of the night as a time for rest and a break from their work. They woke up when the sun rose in the sky and it was light once again.

By and large, the people were happier. They did not have to keep working until they dropped down exhausted. They knew that they had to stop when it got dark and they could see nothing. In this way, their time got splitted into hours of sleep and work equally and they felt much better.

But there was one problem. Since, they could see nothing after sunset, they often fell into ditches and holes. They banged against trees and knocked against people. They could not see where things were kept and broke things. It became quite chaotic!

Then the Creator visited them once again. "Well," he asked, "are things any better now that you have days and nights? Do you feel better after resting all night?"

"Oh yes," they told him. "We feel better and fresh in the morning. But we cannot see when it is dark. So we often get hurt, lose and break things. It is really very difficult after it gets dark. Can't we have the sun for a little while longer? That would make life so much easier for us."

"No," said the Creator, "you cannot have the sun at night. But I shall give you something else to make light for you. Its light will not be as bright as the sun's. But you will be able to see and walk on the roads although, you will not be able to work in your fields. It will give you a nice, soothing light which will make things much easier and stop you from having accidents."

And then, he created the **moon.** It rose in the sky and shone softly at night. People could see but the soothing light did not hurt their eyes or stop them from sleeping. After that it was a happy and comfortable life for man with the bright sun in the day and the glistening moon at night!

The Value Of Tears

It was the month of spring. Flowers bloomed everywhere—red, blue, yellow, orange and white. Birds sang and everyone was happy with a smiling face.

Queen Madhurima woke up, one such morning. She looked out of her window. She saw the flaming maze of colours in the garden. She heard the soft notes of the nightangle and her heart filled with joy.

"May we go into the woods to celebrate the Spring Festival, my Lord?" She asked the king, her husband. He smiled and nodded.

So, Queen Madhurima went to the woods with her friends and attendants. They bathed in the crystal pool. They picked flowers and made garlands. They chased butterflies and sang with the birds. Everyone was happy. In short, they had a wonderful day. Then slowly the daylight faded and the birds flew back to their nests. Queen Madhurima returned to her palace with slow, reluctant steps.

She waited for the king, eager to tell him all about her perfect day in the woods. But he did not come. Seconds turned to minutes and minutes to hours. The moon shone bright. The roads grew quiet but still the king did not arrive. The queen's impatience turned into anger. How could he neglect her like this when she was so eager to tell him about her wonderful day? When the king stood at her door at last, it was nearly midnight.

"What made you so late, my Lord?" she asked in a curt voice.

"The sorrows of the people," answered the king.

"Sorrows? I don't understand you, my Lord. What sorrows?"

"Their problems and difficulties. Who else can help them but the king? I had to listen to their grievances and find solutions."

Queen Madhurima tossed her pretty head. "What a shame to waste such a beautiful day hearing complaints!" The king smiled but said nothing. The same thing happened the next day and the day after.

Finally, the queen spoke to the king about it. "Why is your kingdom so different from the woods?" she asked. "Here inside the palace, we have nothing but sighs and tears. Sorrows and problems. I am sick of it all. I want to be happy. I want nothing but smiles and laughter."

"But that is not possible, Madhurima," the king said gently. "Life is made of both light and darkness, joy and sorrow, laughter and tears. We have to face both. It is just not possible to shut one of them out."

Queen Madhurima shook her head obstinately. "Everything is possible, my Lord. You must proclaim that whoever sheds tears in my kingdom shall be banished forever."

The king looked at her, amazed and hurt. "You are the queen and mother of the people. How can you wish for anything so unkind and unreasonable?"

"I do wish it, and that's all there is to it," she said. "You will not refuse me my wish if you love me."

"So be it," said the king. "But you shall regret it before long, my queen."

The proclamation was made far and wide. People heard it in mute astonishment. How could the queen of the land, supposed to be the mother of her subjects, proclaim anything so heartless and unreasonable? Tears consoled them and made their grief lighter to bear. How could they smile and laugh in the face of grief, loss, pain and sorrow? The number of banished people increased by leaps and bounds. They decided to leave the kingdom when they could not stop their tears.

Seasons tripped by and it was almost a year now. It was spring once again. The woods were ablaze with colour and fragrance.

The birds sang all day. But Queen Madhurima had no time for all these things. Her only son, the prince of the land lay seriously ill. Her heart was as heavy as lead. Doctors from all over the world came to treat him. But it was of no use. When the sun rose the next morning, unfortunately, the little prince was dead. Queen Madhurima was shocked with grief and she cried and cried. It seemed as though, she would never smile again.

The next morning, the king sent for her in his court.

"You have broken your own command, Madhurima," he said in a clear voice. "You must now face banishment."

The queen looked at him in amazement. "But how can the queen of the land be banished, my Lord?" she asked.

"I made the law at your command and a law once made spares nobody. Not even royalty. You must leave this kingdom."

Queen Madhurima was shown out of the royal gates into the deep forest beyond. Tears blinded her as she stumbled along, expecting to be attacked by wild animals. Then she heard voices. All the banished people were there in the forest. They welcomed their queen shared her sorrow. They built a shelter for her.

Days flew by. The people gradually learned to love and respect their banished queen, who seemed to have changed so much. She took her punishment bravely and did not complain. Instead, she spent her time getting to know her banished people and sharing their joys and sorrows. She served and toiled, aided and nursed the people, who had given her a new life.

One bright morning, the king appeared in his golden chariot. Looking around, he saw Queen Madhurima nursing a sick child. Though the child belonged to one of her poor and homeless subject, the child clung to her arms, the arms of a queen! There were tears in her eyes. The queen was crying because while nursing this sick child, she remembered her own son, who had died due to serious illness, some time back. The king was watching it all and asked Madhurima, "Have you learnt the value of tears?"

"I have, my Lord," the queen answered softly. "Then come back to your kingdom with all your banished subjects," said the king.

Ramu Does His Best

Once upon a time, there lived a king whose subjects were good and loyal. But the king was worried because there did not seem to be anybody, who was outstanding in his kingdom. He was sure that not one of them would be of any use if something unexpected happened.

The chief minister was a clever man. But he was growing old and would soon need to retire. The king could not decide, who the next minister should be.

At a time like this, a young boy named Ramu came to the court and begged the king to give him a job. He was a stranger to the place. In fact, not a soul knew anything about him.

"What can you do?" asked the king curiously.

"Oh, anything," Ramu replied. "I really don't mind what the job is."

"Please understand clearly that though I shall give you a job, I shall pay you nothing," said the king. "If you are intelligent, you will find some way of supporting yourself."

"Very well," said Ramu cheerfully. "All I want is a job to do! I shall do my best, sire. Believe me, I shall do my best."

The king consulted his chief minister. The two of them thought of a job which they felt for sure that Ramu would be unable to do. Ramu was told to measure all the roads of the city.

"Think over it, can you manage?" asked the minister, looking at him keenly.

"I shall do my best," said Ramu, confidently.

Ramu was given a set of tapes and measures and was told to get on with his job.

Ramu went to the busiest part of the market and ordered all the vendors to move away so that he could measure the place. The vendors were simply annoyed at first. But their anger turned to dismay when they realised that Ramu had the king's permission to do what he said.

"But how long will it take?" they asked in alarm.

"Can't say," Ramu replied gravely. "Possibly the whole day. It's a big job and I have to do it alone."

"But our business will be ruined!" cried the vendors. "Can you measure the place with all of us here?"

"It will be far more difficult," said Ramu. "Besides, I don't see why I should oblige you."

The vendors offered to pay him a percentage of their profit, if only he would leave them alone.

"Very well, I shall do my best," answered Ramu.

When Ramu went to the king that evening to give him the measurements surveyed during the day, he also took a large bag full of money and gave it to the king.

"Don't tell me you made all this money just by measuring roads!" the king cried in amazement. "And why have you brought it to me? I told you that you could keep what you earned!"

"I have already kept as much as I need," replied Ramu. "The rest belongs to you because I was doing your work."

The king was pleased, but did not say anything.

*****

The minister found another job for Ramu, the next day. He asked Ramu to stand at the bell-tower, the whole day and strike at the bell every hour. Ramu found the new job exceedingly boring. By the time it was two in the morning, Ramu was so bored that he decided to ring the bell five times instead of twice just to see if anything unusual happened. Even if someone came to scold him for the mistake, at least, it would create a diversion!

Now, it so happened that a burglar had decided to rob the palace that very night. He was just gloating over his loot when he heard the bell. He shot up in alarm, when he heard five strokes. Good gracious! Had he taken all that long to steal just half-a-dozen bags of gold coins?

And now, it was almost morning! So many people would be up at five o'clock! Just then, he caught sight of Ramu pacing about below the bell-tower! Was he coming to catch him and take him straight to the king? The burglar ran and fell at Ramu's feet and begged for mercy. He was still clutching a couple of bags in his hand. He gave both to Ramu and begged him to keep quiet. Ramu, though startled, did not show it. He gravely took the bags and warned the burglar never to do such a thing again if he didn't want to spend the rest of his life behind bars.

The next morning, when the king saw the two bags full of gold coins, he was astonished. "Do you mean to say you made all that money in one night just by ringing the bell?" he asked. "I simply don't believe it!"

Ramu was honest and told him the whole story, adding that he had taken only one coin from the bag to pay for his boarding and lodging.

"This money was earned accidentally," said the king. "I don't feel you deserve any credit for it. Your new job will be to sit beside the river the whole day and count the waves."

"Very well, sire, I shall do my best," said Ramu.

*****

Ramu sat in a conspicuous place beside the river, the next morning and would not let any boat pass. "I am doing a job for the king and I cannot be disturbed," he told the people, he had held up. "Besides, if I let you pass, the waves will break and I shall lose count."

The people in the boats were mostly merchants, who were greatly annoyed at the thought of their business suffering on account of being delayed. They gave Ramu large sums of money to let them pass. "Just count double for every broken wave," they said, winking at Ramu. Ramu grinned and nodded.

That evening, Ramu had a large amount of money to hand over along with the illusory count of waves! The king and his old minister were astonished. But when they heard how it had happened, they thought that the broken waves must have made correct counting impossible.

"I am sure there was no mistake," said Ramu with great confidence, "but if you really want to verify it, why don't you count the waves yourself and check?"

The king and his minister realised that Ramu was too smart for them.

"I have a new job for you!" said the king. "You will just sit beside me in the court tomorrow and say nothing. Let me see what you manage to earn."

*****

The next morning, Ramu wore a grand pair of clothes, put on a large turban, and carried a huge empty bag along with a notebook. He managed to sit a little behind the king, who could not see Ramu although the people of the court had a clear view of him. While the king proceeded with his routine task of listening to the grievances of the people, Ramu got up every now and then and pretended to whisper something to the king. He also made a show of writing in his notebook. The people assumed that if they put in a coin or two into Ramu's bag, he would put in a good word for them to the king. As each person passed by, he put some coins into Ramu's bag with a slip containing his name and a special request.

When Ramu saw what was happening, he frowned at them and shook his head. The people thought he was annoyed because they had given him so little. So, they began to put in more and more money. In a short while, Ramu's bag was bursting at the seams! He handed it all to the king at the end of the day.

That evening, Ramu was summoned to the palace. The king smiled at him and patted him on the back. "You are a smart lad, Ramu," he said. "You will be able to share and unburden my duties. My old minister retires tonight and tomorrow, you shall take his place."

After some years, Ramu married the king's only daughter and finally became the king of the land. However, he never failed to "do his best" for the people and ruled kindly, wisely, and well.

When Destiny Decides...

Once upon a time, there lived a rich merchant named Mahipal. He was very proud of his wealth and his position in the society. But though the people were polite with him, no one really liked him very much. This was because Mahipal was often unfair, mean, and unscrupulous about money matters.

Mahipal was fond of showing off his wealth. So he often threw grand parties and banquets, inviting all the important people in town. These were joyous occasions for the poor people, who flocked to his back door and collected all the leftovers.

An orphan boy named Dev lived close to Mahipal's house. Both his parents had died of a sudden illness, leaving him all alone in the world. And no one had volunteered to take care of him. Little Dev slept under the trees at night and lived on the food thrown away by Mahipal's servants. They liked the little boy and always saved some titbits for him.

One morning as Dev sat under a tree eating his breakfast of puffed rice and jaggery, two men passed by talking to each other. One of them was a well-known astrologer. "Look at the cruelty of destiny," said the other man. "Here is Mahipal with more money than he knows what to do with and getting richer everyday. And right across his door is this little boy, fair enough to be a prince, yet living on Mahipal's leftovers."

"Don't let either instance bother you," said the astrologer with a smile. "The wheel of destiny is never still and has its own way of bringing about justice."

"How?" asked the other man curiously.

"You will be surprised if I tell you what fate has in store for these two. It may be years from now, but this little beggar will one day possess Mahipal's entire wealth!"

"Strange!" exclaimed the other man. "But how can that be? Mahipal is not childless. He has a son and a daughter, too. Why should he adopt a beggar?"

"I can't tell you how exactly destiny will bring it about, but I know for certain that it will be so."

Unnoticed by them, at that moment, Mahipal was standing near the window, and overheard the conversation between the two men. At first, he laughed scornfully and said to himself, "Destiny indeed! As if anything on earth would induce me to adopt this beggar boy! They are talking nonsense. Utter nonsense!"

But a feeling of vague uneasiness haunted him from that day. Finally, he made up his mind not to take any chances. Mahipal sent for a hired killer and asked him to take Dev inside a deep forest and kill him there. "And you must show me the bloodstained dagger after you have done the deed. Or else, I shall not pay you," he added.

It was not difficult to take Dev to the forest. He was only four years old and had not learnt to doubt or distrust people. The killer asked Dev to follow him telling the boy, he would show him something wonderful in the forest. Dev cheerfully trotted behind him.

But the killer was, after all, humane and little Dev won his heart completely with his trusting smile. By the time, they reached the middle of the forest, Dev was exhausted and fell asleep in the killer's arms. The killer left him under a tree, killed a fox instead and took the bloodstained dagger to show Mahipal.

*****

Govinda, an old milkman, saw the sleeping child under the tree when he was passing through the forest. He was astonished. How could such a little boy come into the forest all alone? Govinda was a childless man. He had visited all the shrines in the country, beseeching the gods to bless him with a son. He now felt that the boy was a gift from Lord Shiva himself.

He picked up the sleeping child and took him home. His wife was bewildered with joy when she saw the little boy. "Whose child is he?" she asked.

"He is a gift from Lord Shiva," said Govinda.

“He looks like a little angel!” said his wife rapturously. “Are you sure his people won’t come and take him away?”

Dev was awake by now. When he heard them talking, he said, “I have no one and no one wants me either. I would love to stay here if you want me.”

Years flew by. Dev was a young man now, the adored darling of the old couple. He looked after them, the cattle and took over all Govinda’s works. One evening, Mahipal happened to pass by the same forest and his eyes fell on young Dev, who was taking the cattle home. Mahipal recognised him instantly and asked him, who he was.

“I am the son of Govinda, the milkman.”

“Really?” said Mahipal, looking at him closely. “Please take me to your father, will you?”

Dev took him home to Govinda, who was astonished to see Mahipal. The latter’s contempt for poor people was well known and Govinda could not imagine why he was there. But he welcomed Mahipal humbly.

“I understand that this young man is your son, Govinda,” Mahipal said without any preamble.

“Yes sir,” said Govinda.

“But I thought you were childless,” said Mahipal, giving him a sharp look. “I certainly don’t remember being told that you had a son.”

“Lord Shiva decided to be kind to us rather late in life,” agreed Govinda.

“Well, I want an urgent message to be sent home,” said Mahipal. “Could your son carry the letter?”

“Of course sir,” said Govinda. “He will be delighted to do it.”

Mahipal wrote a letter to his son, urging him to poison the bearer of the letter, the moment he arrived there and added that it was extremely important and that there should be no delay.

Dev carried the letter, not knowing what it contained. Before he could reach Mahipal’s house, it grew dark. Dev, who had been walking for hours, was tired. He sat down under a tree to rest for a few minutes. But he was so exhausted that he soon fell asleep.

Just then Ramana, a court-dancer, was passing that way. She stopped in surprise when she saw Dev fast asleep under the tree. He was so very handsome! Ramana wondered who he was. She caught sight of the letter lying beside him. She opened it out of curiosity and read the contents. A mischievous smile lit up her eyes. Ramana hated Mahipal. She had hated him ever since he had grabbed her father's property unlawfully. Here was a wonderful opportunity to pay him back. She opened the letter once again. Mahipal had urged his son to give *veesh* (poison) to the stranger. It so happened that Mahipal's daughter was called Veesha. What a strange coincidence, thought Ramana. The letter was written in red ink. Ramana pricked her finger with a thorn and added a vertical line after Veesh with her own blood, changing the word to *Veesha* in the vernacular language. Veesha was the adored darling of her father. Now she would be married to the man Mahipal was bent on killing!

Dev woke up after a while and hurried to Mahipal's house. Mahipal's son read the letter and called him inside. "Give Veesha to the carrier of my letter," his father had written, adding that there should be no delay. Dev was given a set of new clothes. A priest was sent for, and Dev and Veesha were married in an hour's time.

When Mahipal came home the next day and heard everything, he could not imagine, who had tampered with his letter. Could it have been Dev? Would he dare do such a thing? Besides, how could he have known that his daughter was called Veesha? Mahipal was mad with rage though he kept it to himself.

"I'll still kill you, you beggar!" he muttered to himself. Then he sent for Dev and told him that he should go and worship at the family temple immediately as was the custom in his family. He had already posted a man there with orders to kill anyone, who entered the temple, whosoever it might be.

Dev was about to go inside the temple when Mahipal's son saw him from his window and called out to him. "Where are you going?" he asked Dev.

"To the temple," said Dev. "Father told me to go there at once."

"But how can you go alone? Both of you should worship together," said her brother. "You go and call my sister while I tell the priest that you are coming and see that everything is ready."

"Very well," said Dev, as he went inside the house to call his wife.

When Mahipal saw Dev inside the house, he was enraged. "Haven't you gone to the temple yet?" he shouted. "I told you to go there immediately."

"Your son asked me to take Veesha with me," said Dev. "I've just come to call her."

"And where is my son?" asked Mahipal, turning white.

"At the temple, waiting for us," said Dev.

Mahipal screamed and ran towards the temple. But it was too late. His son lay at the door in a pool of blood. His lifeless eyes seemed as if they were staring at Mahipal accusingly. Mahipal cursed himself and tore his hair. But he was still determined to kill Dev.

*****

A few days later Mahipal brought one small plastic and one metallic basket to his wife. He had poisoned the fruits contained in the metallic basket.

"These are special fruits", he told her. "When we have supper tonight, give the fruits of the metallic basket to your son-in-law, and the ones contained in the plastic basket to me".

"Very well", said his wife and took away the fruits. She was lost in her thoughts, busy with her cooking, when she unknowingly mixed up the contents of the baskets while shifting them onto a single one. She had needed the other basket to stock some vegetables.

She served them both in identical gold plates. Now it so happened that the poisoned fruits went to Mahipal's share.

Dev excused himself and went out for some urgent work. Meanwhile, Mahipal started eating as he thought that Dev might take long.

Mahipal fell in a swoon as soon as he ate the first fruit. He never opened his eyes. The entire house was plunged into grief. Dev inherited

Mahipal's property because there was no male in the family except him. But unlike Mahipal, he lived a life of peace, was generous to all and greatly loved by everyone.

"Do you think it was destiny punishing my father?" Veesha asked her husband, one day.

"I don't know about destiny," said Dev. "But I do know that no good can come of evil. If we lead a good and useful life and do our duty faithfully, we need not fear destiny or any other power."

Veesha agreed and they lived happily ever after.